FROZEN
Worlds

FIRST EDITION

Project Editor Allison Singer; **Assistant Editor** Prerna Grewal; **US Senior** Editor Shannon Beatty;
Art Editors Emma Hobson, Mohd Zishan; **Jacket Editor** Francesca Young;
Jacket Designers Amy Keast, Dheeraj Arora; **DTP Designer** Dheeraj Singh;
Picture Researcher Sakshi Saluja; **Producer, Pre-Production** Nadine King;
Producer Niamh Tierney; **Managing Editors** Laura Gilbert, Monica Saigal; **Managing Art Editors**
Diane Peyton Jones, Neha Ahuja Chowdhry; **Art Director** Martin Wilson; **Publisher** Sarah Larter;
Publishing Director Sophie Mitchell; **Reading Consultant** Linda Gambrell PhD

THIS EDITION

Editorial Management by Oriel Square
Produced for DK by WonderLab Group LLC
Jennifer Emmett, Erica Green, Kate Hale, *Founders*

Editors Grace Hill Smith, Libby Romero, Michaela Weglinski;
Photography Editors Kelley Miller, Annette Kiesow, Nicole DiMella;
Managing Editor Rachel Houghton; **Designers** Project Design Company; **Researcher** Michelle Harris;
Copy Editor Lori Merritt; **Indexer** Connie Binder; **Proofreader** Larry Shea;
Reading Specialist Dr. Jennifer Albro; **Curriculum Specialist** Elaine Larson

Published in the United States by DK Publishing
1745 Broadway, 20th Floor, New York, NY 10019
Copyright © 2023 Dorling Kindersley Limited
DK, a Division of Penguin Random House LLC
23 24 25 26 10 9 8 7 6 5 4 3 2 1
001-333909-June/2023

A catalog record for this book
is available from the Library of Congress.
HC ISBN: 978-0-7440-7219-8
PB ISBN: 978-0-7440-7220-4

DK books are available at special discounts when purchased in bulk for sales promotions, premiums,
fundraising, or educational use. For details, contact: DK Publishing Special Markets,
1745 Broadway, 20th Floor, New York, NY 10019
SpecialSales@dk.com

Printed and bound in China

The publisher would like to thank the following for their kind permission to reproduce their images:
a=above; c=center; b=below; l=left; r=right; t=top; b/g=background
Alamy Stock Photo: Auscape International Pty Ltd / Jean-Paul Ferrero 26-7, Biosphoto / Fabrice Simon 13tr;
Dreamstime.com: Monkeygreen 21tr, 30cl, Andrei Stepanov 8-9, Vampy1 19cb; **naturepl.com:** Norbert Wu 23c;
PunchStock: Digital Vision / Tim Hibo 6-7b; **Shutterstock.com:** Sergey 402 4-5b, Wirestock Creators 18-19

Cover images: *Front:* **Dreamstime.com:** Anastasiya Aheyeva cra, Vladimir Melnikov bl

All other images © Dorling Kindersley
For more information see: www.dkimages.com

For the curious
www.dk.com

FROZEN
Worlds

Caryn Jenner

Contents

The Arctic

The Arctic is a very cold place.

Brrr!
It is at the top of Earth.

The Arctic Ocean
is full of ice.

Arctic

Plants in the Arctic

The land in the Arctic
is rocky.
The ground is frozen.
Many plants
still grow here.

People in the Arctic

These children
live in the Arctic.
They dress warmly
to play in the snow.

Polar Bears

Polar bears live
in the Arctic, too.
These furry animals
like to eat fish.

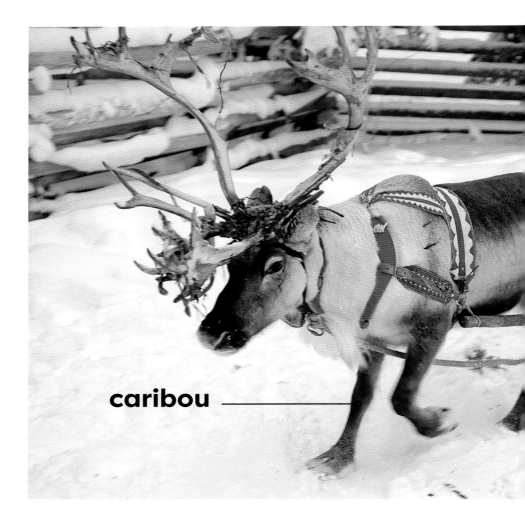

caribou

On the Move

A caribou pulls a sleigh across the snow.

sleigh

Zoom!
Here comes
a snowmobile.

snowmobile

Antarctica

Antarctica is at
the bottom of Earth.

It is even
colder than
the Arctic!

Antarctica

Land in Antarctica

Antarctica has many mountains.
The mountains are covered with snow and ice.

The rest of Antarctica is, too!

Antarctica

Icebergs

Big icebergs float
in the sea.
The icebergs melt.

Drip, drip.

iceberg

Penguins

Emperor penguins
live in Antarctica.

They swim in the cold sea and look for fish to eat.

Sea Animals

Splash!
A whale leaps out
of the water.

A seal watches
from the rocks.

Seasons

The Arctic has
two seasons.
Antarctica does, too.

In summer, it is always sunny. In winter, it is always dark.

Light Show

Sometimes, the night sky lights up in many colors.

What an amazing sight!

Glossary

Antarctica
a cold place at the bottom of Earth

Arctic
a cold place at the top of Earth

iceberg
a huge floating piece of ice in an ocean

sleigh
a wagon that is pulled by an animal over snow

snowmobile
a machine that travels over snow and ice

Index

Quiz

Answer the questions to see what you have learned. Check your answers with an adult.

1. Where is the Arctic?

2. True or False: No plants grow in the Arctic.

3. Where is Antarctica?

4. What are three animals that live in Antarctica?

5. How are the Arctic and Antarctica the same as where you live? How are they different?

1. At the top of Earth 2. False 3. At the bottom of Earth
4. Emperor penguins, whales, and seals 5. Answers will vary